IN THE HALLS OF QUIET STORMS

MOHAMMED ZARAR

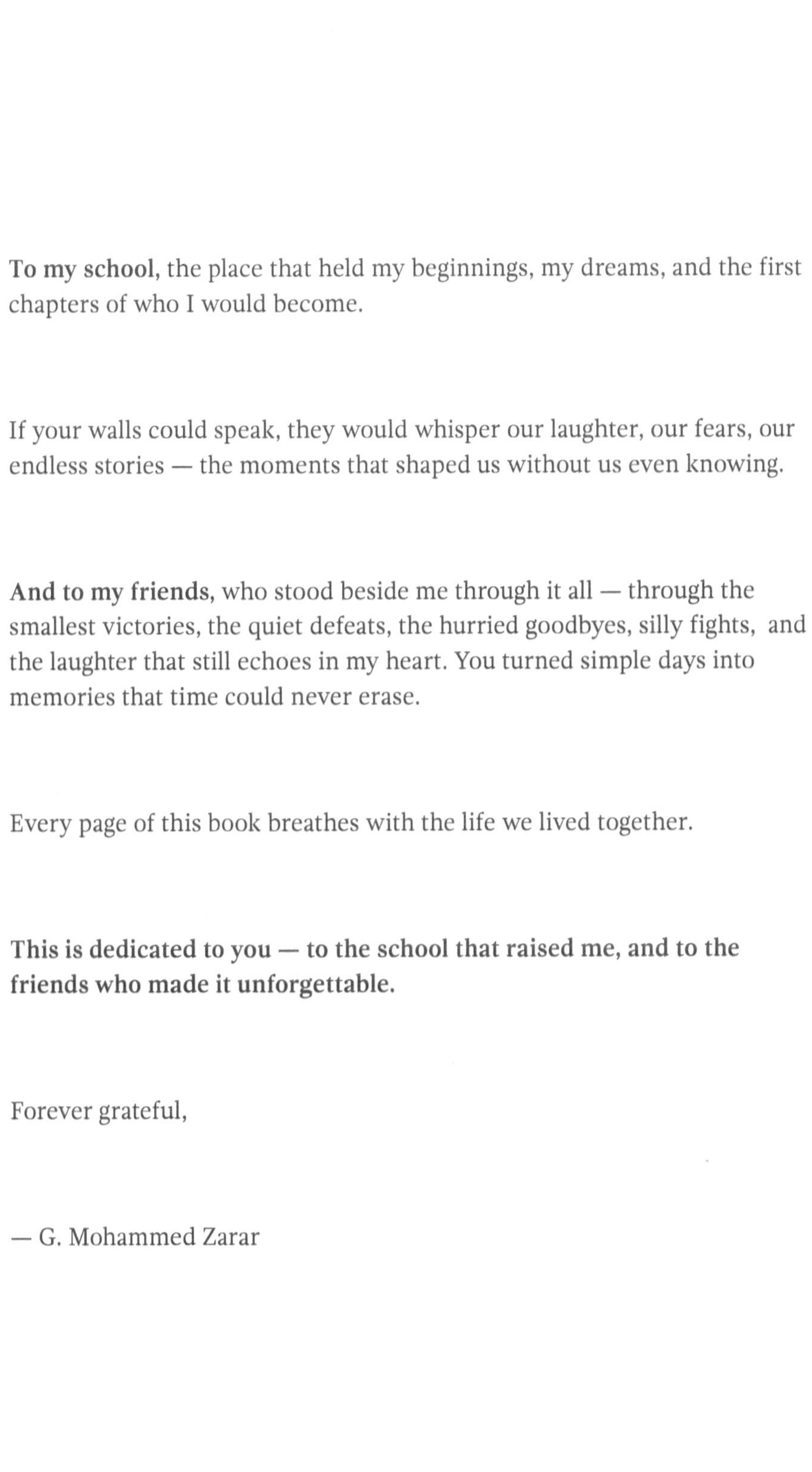

To my school, the place that held my beginnings, my dreams, and the first chapters of who I would become.

If your walls could speak, they would whisper our laughter, our fears, our endless stories — the moments that shaped us without us even knowing.

And to my friends, who stood beside me through it all — through the smallest victories, the quiet defeats, the hurried goodbyes, silly fights, and the laughter that still echoes in my heart. You turned simple days into memories that time could never erase.

Every page of this book breathes with the life we lived together.

This is dedicated to you — to the school that raised me, and to the friends who made it unforgettable.

Forever grateful,

— G. Mohammed Zarar

Contents

Preface

There are some chapters of our lives that we live once, but carry forever.
For me, school was one of them.

This book is not just a collection of memories — it is a piece of my heart. A journey through the corridors where friendships blossomed, dreams were first whispered, and life unfolded in its purest form. From the innocent days of laughter and games, through the silence of unexpected lockdowns, to the bittersweet return to a world forever changed — every word in these pages comes from a place of truth, longing, and love.

I wrote this not just to remember, but to relive.
To honor the carefree mornings, the unspoken promises, the endless playground races, the last-minute exam panics, the whispered secrets across classroom benches.
And to hold onto the faces, the voices, the fleeting moments that time can never truly take away.

This book is for anyone who ever sat under a school tree and dreamed, who ever laughed a little too loud in class, who ever hugged a friend a little tighter before the final bell.
It's a reminder that even when the gates close and the chapters end, some parts of us never really leave. They stay — tucked away in memories, in dreams, in the quiet corners of who we are becoming.

Thank you for stepping into my world.
I hope, as you turn these pages, you find glimpses of your own story too.

— *G. Mohammed Zarar*

Acknowledgements

Some stories are not written alone — they are built with countless hands, hearts, and shared memories.

I am deeply grateful to my family, whose endless support, love, and prayers have been the quiet strength behind every step of this journey.

To my parents — your unwavering faith, sacrifices, and unconditional love are the foundation upon which every dream of mine stands. Without you, none of this would have been possible.

To my sisters — thank you for being my silent cheerleaders, and a constant source of encouragement when I needed it most. Thank you encouraging me and being my side everytime.

To my classmates — you were not just faces in a classroom, but companions through laughter, challenges, dreams, and growing pains. Thank you for standing by me, for sharing moments of pure joy, and for being a part of memories that will forever live in the halls of my heart.

To all my supporters — the friends, mentors, and well-wishers who believed in me even when I doubted myself — your encouragement gave me the courage to bring these memories to life.

To my teachers, who taught me lessons beyond books.

To every reader who finds a part of their own journey within these pages — thank you for walking alongside me through the echoes of these quiet storms.

Above all, I bow my head in gratitude to Allah SWT — the One who blessed me with these memories, this voice, and this opportunity to share a small piece of my soul with the world.

This book is not just mine — it is ours.
For every friend, every smile, every moment that mattered.

ACKNOWLEDGEMENTS

Thank You.
— G. Mohammed Zarar

CHAPTER ONE

"WHISPERS OF A NEW BEGINNING".

It all starts on a quiet, golden morning. The sun streams in gently, as if it knows the weight of the day ahead. You stand at the threshold of something unknown, dressed neatly in clothes that feel too new, too crisp—like they don't belong to you yet. There's a strange stillness in your heart, a calm before the unraveling. A vehicle halts at your doorstep. A stranger steps out—not with menace, but with routine. And just like that, you're ushered into a journey you didn't choose, a path that silently promises to claim the next twelve years of your life. You sit there, watching your home fade from the window, not knowing that a part of you is being left behind with it.Your fingers grip the seat. Your heart stirs uneasily. This is not a vacation. This is not a playdate. This... is your new reality.

As you arrive, unfamiliar walls greet you. Tall gates, loud voices, a playground that doesn't echo with your name. You step in, and everything is different. The smells, the colors, the sounds—it's a collage of chaos stitched together with rules you haven't yet learned.That once carefree child, who only knew the gentle cadence of family life, now stands amidst a crowd of strangers. Your eyes dart from face to face, hoping—desperately—that someone will look like home. But no one does. No one could. You're handed over to a new caretaker. Not your mother's tender hands. Not your father's reassuring nod. Just a smile that's too formal, too distant. They speak softly, but it doesn't carry warmth. It carries duty.

You walk into a classroom. Wooden benches, a dusty blackboard, walls covered in charts that mean nothing to you yet. You take a seat. Front or back—it doesn't matter. You feel alone either way. You try to stay strong. You try not to show what's happening inside you. But your thoughts rebel. They run wild—back to your room, your toys, the half-finished breakfast you didn't touch this morning. You think of your mother's voice calling your name, of your father fixing your collar just right. You blink fast. But the tears come anyway—silent, warm, disobedient..

Then comes the bell. A shrill, unfamiliar sound. Lunch break.

You walk with heavy steps toward the dining space. Around you, laughter blooms, loud and uninviting. You sit at a table of strangers. The food smells different. The taste is foreign. There's no steel plate from home. No one asking you if you want more. But then—someone offers you a piece of their chapati. Another places a sweet near your lunchbox. You look up. A smile meets yours—not quite familiar, but not unkind either. You offer some of your food back. Slowly, the silence breaks. A word, a question, a laugh. Something shifts.

You're still not home. And you won't be for a while.

At last, the veil of unfamiliarity begins to lift. The child, who once stood at the threshold of this new world with hesitant steps and an anxious heart, slowly finds footing. The initial fear, once looming like a shadow, begins to dissolve into acceptance. Eyes that darted around in confusion now begin to settle. There is an effort to blend into the new rhythm, to breathe in the air of a space once unknown, now slowly becoming a part of one's own.

The voice of the teacher—earlier just a distant echo—transforms into a melody of comfort. Every word, every gentle instruction, begins to hold meaning. It is not just noise anymore; it is the beginning of understanding, of connection.

The surroundings, once overwhelming, now invite attention. The colours on the walls, the shapes on the board, the books stacked neatly, even the soft murmur of classmates—all of it starts weaving into a tapestry of belonging.

And time, which once dragged like an endless road, starts slipping away unnoticed. Moments are spent in wonder—in silent observation, in slow discovery. The heart, once burdened with the ache of separation, begins to beat to a calmer tune.

Then comes the final bell. A chime that carries with it not just the end of a school day, but a sweet release. For the little one, it is not merely a sound—it is peace, it is homebound hope. Tiny hands wave goodbye to faces that have already started to mean something. New friends. New beginnings.

The vehicle rolls to a gentle halt at the doorstep of familiarity. There she stands—his mother—the lighthouse in the stormy sea of change. Her eyes search with the same urgency, the same love. The child leaps into her arms with the kind of joy words can hardly hold. That warm embrace, tighter than ever, becomes the healing touch, the safety net, the answer to every unspoken question.

And then, like a dam bursting with emotion, the child begins to speak. Tales of crayons, of bells, of benches and boxes, of teachers and new names—spill out in a flood of excitement. Every word a testament to a day lived, a step taken, a world discovered

As the final tale of the day escapes trembling lips—spoken between bursts of laughter and eyes that shimmer with delight—the school bag is finally cast aside. The heavy shoes are slipped off with relief, the uniform, now creased and tired from the weight of the first day, is peeled away without a second thought. In its place comes the comfort of soft, familiar clothes—the favourite ones, worn countless times, holding the warmth of a hundred carefree moments. A quiet declaration that the little soul is now back in the embrace of where the heart truly belongs.

And then arrives the moment most awaited—the aroma of love wafting from the kitchen. A steel plate, glistening with hot, home-cooked food, awaits on the table. The first bite is not just nourishment—it is a memory, a longing fulfilled. It is the taste of warmth, of affection simmered slowly over the flame of care. Every morsel melts not just in the mouth, but deep within the spirit, comforting the places that felt distant and strange just hours ago

Around lies the peace of home—unspoken, unquestioned. The walls no longer echo with silence but with stories, comfort, and love and as the child curls into a familiar corner, the first day gently fades into memory. A day that began with trembling fingers and anxious eyes now rests in the heart as a chapter of courage, growth, and discovery.

The first day ends—not with a full stop, but with a quiet promise. A promise that tomorrow will be easier. That what was once unfamiliar is already becoming a part of the journey. And the heart, now fuller than ever, finally finds its calm. It's not the end of the ache. But it is the whisper of a new beginning.

CHAPTER TWO

"SETTLING INTO THE NEW RYTHM OF LIFE".

A new day slowly unfolds. The soft rays of the morning sun stretch across the room, gently nudging the world awake. Inside a quiet home, a mother walks into her child's room with a familiar rhythm. Her steps are light, her heart full of understanding. She sits by the bedside, gently brushing the child's hair away and whispering the words meant to comfort: "Wake up, my little one. It's time to get ready."

But beneath the blankets, the child stirs reluctantly, clinging to the warmth of home, to the peace of familiar surroundings. The thought of returning to school—the still-new space filled with unfamiliar sounds and expectations—feels overwhelming again. The heart longs to stay wrapped in the known, close to love, close to comfort.

The mother senses it all without the child having to say a word. With a soft smile and a reassuring tone, she says, "There's a holiday tomorrow. Just today, only one more day to get through." It's a small sentence, but it carries enough strength to lift the child from that cocoon of hesistance

Slowly, the child sits up, eyes heavy with sleep and heart heavier with reluctance. The uniform waits neatly on the chair, and breakfast is placed lovingly on the table. The child eats quietly—not because of hunger, but because it's what needs to be done. The clock ticks, and the vehicle arrives. With a small sigh, the child walks out—back to that place which is slowly turning from unknown to known.

And then, something shifts

As the child steps into the classroom, it doesn't feel as strange anymore. The once-intimidating walls now feel a bit more welcoming. The desks, the boards, the faces—they've started to become part of a growing rhythm. The fear of speaking up slowly fades. Conversations begin, hesitations melt away, and what was once silence is replaced by laughs

Throughout the day, the child finds joy in little things—raising a hand to answer a question, nodding along during lessons, even helping a classmate. There's a new sense of ease, of being seen and understood. The connections grow stronger, the bonds slowly forming..

When the lunch break arrives, it brings with it something special. Sitting in a circle with new friends, sharing food, exchanging smiles—this becomes the highlight of the day. Simple conversations turn into joyful chatter. They laugh about little things, tell stories that don't make sense but feel important, and find comfort in each other's presence.

In that moment, the child isn't just a student in a new school. The child is part of something—part of a group, a circle, a new kind of family. The school doesn't feel distant anymore. It starts feeling like a second home.

What started as a day full of reluctance ends with a heart that is a little braver, a little lighter. There's still a long way to go, but today was different. Today marked a small but meaningful shift—a step forward in building something lasting.

And that makes all the difference.

And so, as the days quietly pass, a gentle rhythm begins to take hold. What once seemed daunting and unfamiliar slowly starts to feel natural—almost second nature. The early morning wake-ups, once met with sleepy resistance, now come with a quiet sense of purpose. The uniform, once stiff and foreign, now feels like part of an identity. The school bag, the shoes, the routine—all of it begins to blend into the background of something greater taking form

The child who once clung to the edge of home now steps into the school gates with a steady heart. That nervousness, which once echoed in every uncertain glance and shy step, slowly fades. In its place grows confidence—quiet, steady, and strong. There's a sense of belonging now. Familiar faces greet each other with genuine smiles. Teachers are no longer just guides—they become mentors, comforters, and motivators. Classmates transform into companions, and then, into friends..

The classroom, once a place of silence and observation, fills with chatter and questions. Curiosity flows freely, laughter bubbles up often, and each lesson begins to feel like a story being added to the book of life. The once-intimidating blackboard is now a space of exploration. There's pride in solving a problem, joy in participating, and comfort in being part of a group where one's voice matters.

Outside the classroom, the playground becomes a world of its own—a space where bonds are strengthened through games and giggles. New games are invented on the spot, rules are changed with a laugh, and victories are shared as joyfully as the defeats. The echoes of running footsteps, the shouts of encouragement, the playful teasing—all blend into memories being created in real time.

And gradually, without even realizing it, the child finds themself completely immersed in this world. School is no longer something separate—it has become a part of daily life. A space to learn, to grow, to fall and get up again. A place where every day is a new page, and every moment is a brushstroke on the canvas of early memories.

This is how the new beginning unfolds—not with one grand event, but with countless small moments. Moments that, together, shape a journey. From hesitation to comfort, from quiet to laughter, from a stranger in a new place to a person who belongs.

And just like that, playschool comes to an end.

There were moments of mess, moments of magic, and everything in between. From storytime circles to splashy paint days, from puzzles to playground adventures—it was all part of learning through joy.

CHAPTER THREE

"ADAPTING IN SILENCE, EVOLVING WITH GRACE."

There's a tender ache in growing up — a quiet moment when a child leaves behind the colors of playschool and walks into the structured rhythm of primary school. It isn't loud or celebrated, but it lingers in memory like a faint scent of a crayon box long forgotten.

The day begins with the same morning sun, yet everything feels unfamiliar. The uniform, though similar in shade, now has sharper edges, neatly stitched collars, and shoes that seem to echo louder on the floor. The little fingers, once used to holding a caregiver's hand tightly, now clutch a bag slightly heavier — not just with books, but with the weight of transition.

A sibling walks along, offering a quiet comfort. Their presence feels like a half-remembered lullaby, softly assuring, "You're not alone." The vehicle waiting outside hums a different tune today — not the same cheerful route with the same trees and turns. The roads twist into unknown paths, the outside world racing past windows like frames from a new story.

And then it appears — the school. Taller. Grander. Unfamiliar.

The gates seem to stretch towards the sky. Children of all heights, all voices, whirl around like a windstorm of energy. The little one stands at the edge, eyes wide, heart thudding gently, trying to understand where to belong in this new universe. A hand reaches out — not a parent's this time, but someone new. A teacher, warm-eyed and welcoming, leads them to a room where new beginnings await.

It feels like déjà vu — new faces, new walls, a new nameplate on the door. But this time, the heart knows a little more. It remembers what it felt like to start fresh. And so, it doesn't tremble as much.

A quiet introduction. A notebook handed over. A name spoken in front of strangers. And then comes recess — a playground stretching far and wide, filled with voices that seem older, faster, louder. The child stands still for a moment, letting it all sink in. The slide is taller. The laughter unfamiliar. But beneath the awe lies something else — resilience.

Everything has changed, yet something within stays steady — a little heartbeat that whispers, "I've done this before. I can do it again."

It is in these small, silent steps that childhood grows. Not in leaps, not in shout but in soft, graceful transitions. In the courage to walk into a room full of strangers and smile anyway

Days drift by like clouds across a gentle sky — slow, soft, and unnoticed until you look back. What began as a single, nervous step into the gates of primary school becomes a journey of countless tiny moments stitched together. A journey so delicate, so full of firsts, that only time can reveal how much has changed.

The oversized uniform that once felt stiff now feels like a second skin. The new shoes, which once made awkward clicks on the school floor, now move with ease through corridors lined with memories. The classroom, once a world of strangers and silence, becomes a space filled with laughter, whispered secrets, and familiar faces that slowly grow into a circle of trusted friends.

Each morning greets the little one with routine — the bag packed with books, the water bottle filled, the tiffin lovingly placed. But with every passing day, something more gets packed — confidence. Without knowing it, the child has been learning not just to read and write, but to belong

And just when comfort begins to bloom in full, the first year nears its end. But it doesn't fade away quietly. It presents a new challenge — the first exam. A moment that feels both exciting and terrifying. It's not just another classroom activity. It's a test, a real one, with silence, with rules, and with no one allowed to whisper help. A room that usually echoes with laughter now sits frozen in pin-drop quiet. Desks are spaced out. Sheets of white paper are placed. And then, it begins.

At first, all is well. The pencil moves confidently. Then comes that question — the one the little mind doesn't understand. Eyes scan it once, twice, again. The words don't make sense. Panic begins to rise. The hands that once flipped pages with ease now tremble. The classroom feels too quiet. The question too loud. And without warning, tears — slow, silent tears — find their way down flushed cheeks.

It's not just the question. It's the fear of not knowing. The fear of trying and failing. The fear of being alone in that moment. But then, like a calm breeze after a storm, comes a quiet presence — the teacher.

No answers are given. No rules are broken. Just a soft voice and a gentle gaze.

"Breathe. Don't worry. Read it again. Think slowly. You know more than you think."

And somehow, those words build a bridge. Between fear and courage. Between confusion and clarity. The pencil lifts again. The child reads the question one more time — this time, not in fear, but with belief.

A quiet belief that perhaps, they do know this. And slowly, the answer forms. It's written down — not perfectly, but bravely. And that bravery matters more than anything.

That small success lights something inside. It isn't loud, but it's lasting. It tells the child — "You can do this. You did this."

Note from the author:

The following chapters are gonna have a nostalgic, simple tone different from the previous ones.

CHAPTER FOUR

"DOING WHAT FEELS RIGHT".

Dear reader,

Among all the pages I've turned in my journey of school life, this one—this precious chapter—stands apart. Not because it was filled with academic brilliance or life-changing events, but because it was filled with the purest form of happiness I've ever known. A kind of happiness that didn't know it was fleeting. A happiness that was raw, innocent, and real.

This chapter is all about my time in Grade 4 and 5. The most cherished years. A time where the word "stress" didn't exist in our dictionary. Where studies quietly slipped into the background, and joy took the centre stage. These were the years when school life was less about books and more about bonding. It wasn't about competing—it was about connecting.

I remember walking into the classroom each morning with a wide smile and a carefree heart, already excited about what we'd laugh about today. The chalk fights, the secret pass-around notes, the whispers during lectures, the never-ending games during lunch breaks—they were not just incidents; they were moments that would shape my heart forever.

Those were the years when being chosen for an event, an annual day dance, or an inter-school competition meant the world to us. We would practice for hours, mess up the steps, laugh uncontrollably, and still feel like stars on the big stage. I still remember the thud of my heart when I was made an office bearer for the first time. Wearing that badge was more than just responsibility—it was pride. It was a declaration that I was now someone with authority, however small, and it felt enormous back then.

There were no smartphones, no social media, no phone numbers and yet, we made the best memories. We clicked pictures in our minds and etched them in our hearts. We never knew that one day, we wouldn't see each other again like we used to.

We never imagined something like a "lockdown" would come—a silent villain that would separate us from our closest friends without even a chance to say goodbye. No last hugs. No farewell tears. Just a sudden distance that couldn't be measured in kilometers.

Still, in this very moment—as I write Chapter 4—I feel everything. The warmth of friendship. The echo of laughter. The ringing bell that once felt like music to my ears. School, during those years, wasn't just a routine. It was life. A better life. Friends became family—the kind you didn't realize you were so lucky to have until it was all gone.

I remember how we giggled in the middle of a serious class, annoyed the teachers to the core, and still somehow got away with it. The way we rushed out during breaks like we were running from jail. The way the PT sir would yell at us for running in the corridors, and we'd smile slyly, already planning the next escape.

And then there were those rules... oh, how we broke them! Not out of rebellion, but in pursuit of joy. We didn't realise it then, but in those little rule-breaks, we were building the strongest memories of our lives

Even exams didn't scare us back then. We'd scribble down what we knew, and for the rest—well, we trusted luck and each other. Everything was lighter, easier, happier. We'd scribble down what we knew, and for the rest—well, we trusted luck and each other. Everything was lighter, easier, happier.

Then came the sports days—grand, loud, and unforgettable. We cheered for our teams until our throats went sore and even when our team lost, the bonding was worth every scream. I still remember the proudest moments—when we stood on stage during inter-school competitions, clutching certificates or even just applause, feeling seen and appreciated by our teachers and principal. Recognition in those moments felt bigger than any reward.

Looking back, I realise those days weren't perfect—but they were ours. Pure. Unfiltered. And irreplaceable.

So, dear reader, as you turn this page with me, I hope it stirs something within you too. Maybe a smile. Maybe a tear. Maybe just a memory of your own golden corridor—of friendships that felt like home, and moments that made school more than just a place.

Because for me, this chapter isn't just about nostalgia. It's a reminder of who we were, when life was simpler, and our hearts were fuller.

Be prepared, dear readers, for the next chapter—one that marks a turning point.

For the students of our generation, it wasn't just a new chapter—it was a strange, uncertain, and at times, painfully depressing phase of our lives. A time when everything familiar was suddenly out of reach.

When laughter in school corridors was replaced with silence at home. When friendships felt distant even though hearts were close. This wasn't how we imagined growing up. But this... this was our reality.

CHAPTER FIVE

"THE SHIFT WITHIN".

There stands the most unexpected chapter, a chapter so silent yet so loud, so unimaginable that even now, when we look back, it feels unreal. It was never meant to be part of our school stories, the ones filled with bustling corridors, shared giggles, and whispered secrets. It all began just when everything seemed so beautifully ordinary.

Grade 5 was drawing to a close, and the promise of summer hung in the air like the sweetest melody. There were plans scattered everywhere—in whispered conversations about sleepovers, in excited talks of family trips, in the simple joy of knowing you would have endless afternoons to do absolutely nothing. It was all there, ready, waiting at the edge of the last exam bell. And then, as sudden as a bolt of lightning in a clear blue sky, the news came crashing in. "Lockdown has been imposed. A curfew declared to curb the virus."

The words didn't settle at first. They floated around, heavy but not yet real. How could anything so big, so world-changing, happen to us, to the little world we had built with our friends, our laughter, our dreams?

For a few long hours after hearing the news, there was only confusion. Minds too young to understand tried to piece together what this truly meant. At first, it felt like maybe it was just for a few days. Maybe things would be fine again by the weekend. Maybe we would still meet, still laugh, still plan. But slowly, almost cruelly, reality began to sink in. The summer plans were the first to crumble—one by one, they disappeared, like footprints wiped away by a sudden wave. No meetups. No travel. No running out into the streets with bicycles and ice creams and dreams. Instead, there was only the house. The same four walls that once felt warm and safe now began to feel too quiet, too still. The people you thought you'd see every day—the friends who knew all your jokes, who shared all your silly fears and little victories—suddenly felt oceans away.

And then came the real silence, not the silence of a room, but the silence of missing voices, missing faces, missing moments that you didn't even know were so important until they were gone. You kept looking at your phone, expecting some message to arrive that would fix it all, but instead, the days began to blur together.

Home became the world now. The sounds outside—the school bell, the bus honks, the afternoon games—were replaced by the ticking of clocks and the faint hum of news channels in the background. For a while, you waited, holding on to the belief that any day now things would return. That maybe, just maybe, you would still get to run back into the arms of your old life. But as the days stretched into weeks, and weeks into months, a quiet truth began to settle in your heart.

Without even realizing it, you had crossed an invisible line—the line where childhood, in its purest form, ended. The carefree, thoughtless days of rushing through corridors, whispering in classrooms, sharing silly smiles across the benches, were now tucked away, safe only in memory.

The world outside had changed. And so had you. You learned, perhaps for the very first time, that sometimes goodbyes don't come with warnings. Sometimes they are just a silent closing of a door you didn't even realize you had walked through. That summer, what you lost wasn't just a vacation. It was a part of your youth, of your innocence—a part that would never quite return in the same way again.

CHAPTER SIX

"No More Illusions".

And so began the next chapter — a chapter no one had prepared us for. A chapter that didn't announce itself loudly but slowly seeped into every corner of our lives, until we no longer recognized the world we lived in. Life, as we knew it, did not resume. It shifted, almost reluctantly, into a strange new rhythm that none of us understood, but all of us had to follow. The days that once overflowed with movement—the ringing bells, the morning scramble to catch the bus, the familiar chatter of friends waiting at the gate—were suddenly replaced by days of stillness. The calendar moved forward, but we remained stuck, as if time itself had become lazy, dragging its feet.

Then came the announcement we feared yet expected: school would not reopen. Not after summer, not even after autumn. Everything was to be done from home. The very word 'school' began to change in our minds—it no longer meant corridors and playgrounds and noisy classrooms. It meant a bright screen, a meeting link, a camera button. The first day of online classes felt strange, surreal. There was no scent of freshly sharpened pencils, no last-minute rush to pack bags, no noise at the gates. Just you, sitting quietly in a corner of the house, your books spread out on the dining table or maybe on the bed, staring at a glowing screen with dozens of tiny faces looking back at you. Some faces smiled, some waved, some looked as lost as you felt.

The teachers tried their best—smiling wider, speaking louder, trying to fill the strange void that stretched between us all. But the magic wasn't there. No matter how many classes we attended, no matter how many assignments we completed, something was missing. It wasn't just about education. It was about life. There were no side glances exchanged with friends when a teacher said something funny. No stolen jokes passed on slips of paper. No bursts of laughter when someone dropped their books noisily. It was learning without life. School without soul. A hollow version of the world we once knew.

At first, it seemed easier—less strict, less exhausting. But soon the weight of it began to settle on our shoulders in ways we hadn't expected. We missed raising our hands and feeling the air of the classroom. We missed those moments when the teacher turned to write on the board and the whole class would whisper hurriedly. We even missed the punishments, the last-minute homework, the running to catch the school bus. We missed it all, because it wasn't just about learning. It was about living.

And so, the days grew longer. Every morning blended into the next. There was no clear line between a Monday and a Sunday. Every meal felt the same. Every hour stretched endlessly, and yet somehow, the weeks slipped away quietly, unnoticed. Birthdays came and went without the sound of friends singing off-key. Festivals passed without school decorating the halls with lights and laughter. Even victories—small achievements in online tests, finishing assignments—felt hollow without someone to high-five, without someone to pat you on the back and grin.

Some days, you sat by the window and stared at the empty streets, remembering how they once bustled with life. How every road seemed to carry the voices of children running to school, how every park used to echo with laughter in the evenings. Now, it was just silence. A silence that wasn't peaceful. It was heavy. It made you ache in places you didn't know existed before. And slowly, you realized it wasn't just the noise you missed. It was the presence. The life. The feeling of belonging to something bigger than yourself.

As time passed, you grew used to the online world. You attended classes. You completed homework. You even smiled sometimes at the screen. But a part of you always remained distant, quietly waiting for the day when life would finally feel real again. You held onto hope, stubbornly, desperately, that someday you would walk back into school and find it exactly as you left it. The desks would still have the same carvings. The walls would still echo the same old laughter. The friends would still be waiting where you had left them, as if time had frozen and was only waiting for your return.

But deep down, a quiet, painful understanding had already begun to settle in your heart. Things would not be the same again. You had crossed an invisible line. A line between the life you once knew and the life you now had to learn to live. Childhood was no longer a place you lived in every day. It was slowly becoming a memory. A precious, untouchable memory. And so, Chapter 6 was not about learning new lessons from books. It was about learning life's hardest, quietest lessons—patience, loss, longing, and the strange, heavy beauty of memories that can only be revisited, but never relived.

And so, after what felt like an endless stretch of days, after a year and a half of living in repetition, of waking up to the same walls, the same screens, the same muted birthdays and festivals, something changed. One morning, the familiar flash of news headlines appeared again—not announcing another extension, not another lockdown, but something different. Something we had almost given up hoping for. "Schools set to reopen," the headline read, bold and unbelievable. But there was a catch. Things wouldn't go back to how they were. Not fully. There were new words stitched into the announcement—"new norms," "social distancing," "mandatory face masks," "hand sanitizers," "temperature checks." It sounded more like preparing for a hospital visit than walking into a school.

It felt awkward, almost unreal. You imagined walking into your school and not recognizing the world you had once known so well. How could laughter survive behind masks? How could friendships bloom six feet apart? How could a place that once symbolized freedom now come with so many invisible barriers? Yet, this was the new normal. And somewhere inside, we knew—we had waited too long, missed too much, to turn away now. Even if it was different. Even if it felt strange. It was a chance to reclaim a piece of the life we had lost. A chance to walk back, even if the path had changed. The school gates would open again—not to the world we left behind, but to a world we would now have to learn to call home once more.

And so, as Chapter 6 drew to its slow, heavy close, it left behind not just the memory of the long, quiet waiting, but also the uncertain, flickering hope that perhaps—just perhaps—beginnings could still happen, even after the longest, most painful goodbyes.

CHAPTER SEVEN

"When Empty Classrooms Breathed Again"

The day finally arrived. A day that for so long had only lived in dreams and blurry hopes. You put on your uniform again, though it felt a little tighter now, a little unfamiliar, as if time had woven invisible years into the fabric. You tied your shoelaces with hands that had once done it without thought, now feeling a strange nervousness you couldn't explain. The mask hung from your face, not just covering your mouth and nose, but somehow hiding the part of you that once smiled freely. A small bottle of sanitizer sat in your pocket like a new compulsory friend. Temperature checks awaited at the gates, where once only friends did.

The bus ride—or the walk to school—felt silent, too quiet, as if everyone was holding their breath. And when you reached the gates, it hit you harder than you expected.
You were back.
But not to the school you had left behind.
The walls looked the same. The buildings stood where they always had. The trees still swung in the breeze. And yet, somehow, everything was different.

The faces you saw were no longer the same. Friends who had once been the very center of your world now looked different—taller, older, somehow distant. Some faces you barely recognized anymore, changed not just by time, but by the distance life had forced between you. The familiar voices that once filled the corridors with endless chatter now sounded quieter, deeper, a little more careful. Even the laughter—when it came—felt softer, less wild, as if it had forgotten how to be loud and reckless.

The groups had shifted. Some friendships that once seemed unbreakable now felt awkward, strained, standing there with forced smiles and unsure eyes. New friendships had formed too, somewhere in the lost months, ones you hadn't been a part of. And that hurt in a quiet, aching way that you couldn't put into words. It wasn't anyone's fault. It was just time. Time had moved, and so had people. You had changed too—you could feel it in the way you hesitated before speaking, in the way you searched faces for familiar sparks and sometimes didn't find them.

Classes resumed. Teachers spoke. Lessons were taught. But nothing really picked up exactly where it had left off. There were empty seats where some faces were supposed to be—friends who had moved away, friends who had chosen different paths. Their absence was louder than the silence itself. You sat in classrooms where memories clung to the walls like invisible paintings, but now the colors seemed faded. You laughed sometimes, you smiled often, but somewhere inside, there was always this quiet voice whispering,

"It's not the same anymore."

And that was the hardest lesson you learned—not the one written in books, but the one etched slowly across your heart. That sometimes you can return to a place, but not to a time. That sometimes the places you loved remain, but the people, the moments, the life that once filled them, quietly change when you aren't looking.

Chapter 7 wasn't about sadness, though it carried sadness in its arms. It was about growing up, about learning that life moves even when you're standing still. That change doesn't always come with a bang—sometimes it seeps in quietly, showing itself only when you try to return to the way things were. And yet, hidden inside all that change, there was still something beautiful. New friendships waiting to be discovered. New memories waiting to be made. A new version of you, quietly emerging from the old one, stronger and softer at the same time.

Looking back now, it all feels like a story written in invisible ink—moments that once burned so brightly, now glowing faintly in the corners of our memories. We grew up without realizing it. Somewhere between the first headline and the last goodbye, somewhere between the endless waiting and the cautious return, we changed. We learned that life doesn't pause, even when our hearts want it to. We learned that time moves quietly, reshaping everything we thought was permanent. We lost things we thought we would always have—unfiltered laughter, reckless hugs, the easy comfort of old friends. And yet, in their place, we found new things—new courage, new beginnings, a deeper understanding of how fragile and beautiful life truly is.

School was never just about books and lessons. It was about friendships, laughter, chaos, and dreams stitched into every hallway and every corner. And even though the faces changed, even though the voices deepened, even though everything felt a little different when we returned, the memories stayed. Untouched. Safe. Ours forever.

Maybe that's what growing up really is—not forgetting, not moving on, but carrying all of it with you. The old, the new, the beautiful, the broken. Every chapter, every change, every heartbeat. Carrying it gently in your heart... and learning to smile anyway.

CHAPTER EIGHT

"A New Kind of Normal".

The world, slowly and uncertainly, began to find its way back to normal. The empty streets filled again with the noise of life, the parks found their laughter once more, and the air felt a little lighter after carrying so much silence for so long.

Returning to school after everything felt like stepping into a half-forgotten dream. The classrooms stood where we had left them, the walls still bore the faded charts and notices pinned long ago, but the air was heavier, filled with memories of what we had lost. Walking through the corridors felt both familiar and foreign, like flipping through an old photo album where the faces were the same, yet something had quietly shifted.

The desks were spaced wider now. The chatter was softer. The jokes were still there, but they often ended with nervous glances, as if laughter itself needed permission. Masks slowly came off over time, but some part of us remained guarded, carrying the invisible lessons of distance and loss. Teachers tried their best to bring back the spirit—calling out names, encouraging answers, pushing us into a routine that once felt effortless but now needed to be learned all over again.

Exams returned too, but they weren't the terrifying monsters they once seemed. After months of isolation, even the stress of an exam felt strangely welcome, a sign that life was beginning to stitch itself back together. Sitting in a hall with rows of students, scribbling answers under the ticking clock, felt like a privilege now—a strange kind of joy hidden inside the pressure.

We found ourselves smiling at small things—the creak of a chair, the hurried flipping of pages, the frantic last-minute revisions whispered under our breath. The things we once took for granted had now become treasures we held quietly inside.

School events started trickling back too. Slowly, hesitantly at first. The first sports day after lockdown wasn't grand, but it was loud enough to feel real. We ran across the fields, our legs heavy from long months of stillness, our hearts racing not just from exertion but from sheer gratitude. The cheers were a little less wild, the crowds a little thinner, but every race, every fall, every medal meant more than ever before. It wasn't just about winning anymore—it was about being there, about feeling the air rush past our faces, about standing at the starting line with friends once more.

Annual days, talent shows, small gatherings—all returned, though in simpler forms. There were fewer performances, fewer decorations maybe, but there was more heart. Every skit performed, every dance stepped awkwardly on stage, every line forgotten halfway through a speech was met not with embarrassment, but with pride. We had waited so long for these moments. We had missed them so dearly. It didn't matter if everything wasn't perfect. We were there. Together. Breathing the same air, sharing the same laughter, making new memories to patch up the spaces that the lockdown had left empty.

And yet, even as we laughed and celebrated, we couldn't help but notice the changes. Some familiar faces were missing. Some friends had moved away. Some sat in different classrooms now, their journeys having taken unexpected turns. The innocence we once wore like a second skin was thinner now, worn and patched in places. We were still children—but children who had seen the world fall silent, and rise again.

We learned, slowly, painfully, beautifully, that life never goes back. It only moves forward, carrying the old scars and the new hopes side by side. We weren't trying to return to what we had before. We were learning to build something new—with softer words, tighter hugs, longer laughter. We were learning that even though everything had changed, some things—friendship, joy, dreams—found a way to survive, to return, to grow again.

And so, we moved through the classrooms with a new kind of wonder, sat for exams with a new kind of courage, played our games with a new kind of hunger, and celebrated our school events with a heart that knew what it meant to lose—and what it meant to find the way back again.

We were not who we had been.
But maybe, just maybe, we were something even stronger now

CHAPTER NINE

"THE RISE OF RESPONSIBILITY".

The days flew by as we adjusted ourselves to the new normal, trying to find the rhythm that had once come so naturally. As everything slowly settled back into place—the crowded corridors, the noise of classrooms, the familiar chaos of daily school life—something else began to creep in. The seriousness of studies. It was Grade 9 now—a time when school was no longer just about memories and moments but about expectations and responsibilities.

The pressure came from all sides—teachers reminding us of the importance of marks, parents nudging us to leave behind the playful world of masti and focus on the future. But it wasn't easy. It didn't feel natural. Just a year ago, we were learning to laugh again, to rebuild the friendships we had almost lost during the long silence of lockdown. Just when the bonds had reformed, when the halls once again echoed with the missed-out laughter and long conversations, we were asked to quieten it all down. To swap the noise of friendship for the silence of textbooks. To trade carefree joy for disciplined schedules. It felt unfair, almost cruel. The time we were supposed to have lived fully had been taken from us. And now, when we finally found our smiles again, we were asked to put them away, to chase grades instead of memories.

We tried. We really did. We clicked our pens a little more carefully, underlining notes with colors that screamed seriousness, setting alarms for early morning revisions that almost always ended in snoozed dreams. We made timetables that looked perfect on paper—hours allotted to subjects, neatly divided like slices of cake. But our hearts weren't so neatly organized. Somewhere between solving equations and memorizing dates, we still longed for the unfinished laughter, for the games that were cut short too soon, for the silly, meaningless talks that somehow meant everything.

There were days when we sat together after school, books open in front of us but conversations drifting toward plans of "one last match" or "one small celebration." There were evenings when we promised ourselves we would go straight home and study, only to find ourselves wandering in groups, trying to hold on to a world that was slipping through our fingers. The pressure was real—marks mattered now, future dreams were built from these very days—but it was almost as if our hearts were protesting silently.
"Let us live a little longer," they whispered.
"We lost so much already."

Teachers, too, changed. The same teachers who once smiled indulgently at our mischief now frowned at every slip, every distraction. Parents who once laughed along with our stories of classroom chaos now sat us down at dinner tables with serious talks of board exams and career paths. The world around us demanded focus, demanded that we grow up faster than we were ready for. And maybe, deep down, we understood. But understanding doesn't make letting go any easier.

We were caught in between—a tug of war between yesterday and tomorrow. A part of us still wanted to race down corridors without worrying about tomorrow's test. A part of us still wanted to sit under the old tree in the playground, talking about nothing, dreaming about everything. But the clock ticked louder now. Every month felt shorter. Every exam felt heavier. Every careless moment felt like a gamble we couldn't afford anymore.

This was the beginning of a quieter, heavier chapter of school life.
One where memories still glimmered at the edges, but dreams of the future stood tall in the center.
One where we learned—slowly, painfully—that sometimes growing up doesn't ask for your permission.
It just happens. It just comes, demanding that you leave behind things you weren't ready to let go of.

And even as we tried to laugh, tried to play, tried to hold on to the last golden threads of childhood, we knew—

A new kind of seriousness had crept into our lives.
And this time, it wasn't just a passing phase.
It was the beginning of a race we would now have to run.

And yet, somewhere deep inside, hidden beneath the weight of expectations and the seriousness of new beginnings, a small part of us still held on to the past. A part that still remembered what it felt like to laugh without counting minutes, to play without watching the clock, to dream without fear of failing. Even as we opened our books with determination, even as we filled pages with hurried notes and careful underlines, there remained a quiet corner of our hearts that refused to forget the lost days. The days when life was simple, when friendships were loud, when joy came without a price. And maybe that little part—the one that still carried the laughter, the chaos, the memories—was what kept us human, even as the race ahead grew faster and the world asked us to run.

CHAPTER TEN

"The Final Chapter"

Amidst the constant balancing of studies and the stolen moments of fun, we found ourselves standing at the doorway of the final chapter of our school life — Grade 10. The last year. The last stretch of a journey that had once felt endless, now slipping through our fingers faster than we were ready for. It was a year heavy with firsts and lasts, a year that carried the weight of growing up and the ache of letting go. One last time to sit beside our friends without wondering where life would take us next. One last time to run across the playgrounds without the burden of tomorrow on our shoulders. One last time to laugh till our sides ached, to shout across classrooms, to hold onto friendships that had been our second family for so long.

This was the year of 'lasts.' The last sports day where we ran not to win, but to savor every second. The last annual day, where the stage lights blurred not because of nerves, but because of unshed tears. The last Teachers' Day, when we looked at our teachers with a gratitude too big for words. The last festive celebrations, where every smile hid the quiet realization that soon, all of this would become memory. We cheered louder, laughed harder, and clung tighter to every event, every gathering, every stolen moment—because deep down, we knew. This was it. This was the final chapter we would write together before life turned the page for us, scattering us across different streams, different cities, different dreams.

We tried to capture everything, to hold on to each moment a little longer, as if by doing so we could slow down time. But time, as always, was slipping quietly through the cracks, carrying us forward whether we were ready or not. The pressure of studies grew heavier with each passing day. Board exams loomed ahead like a mountain we had no choice but to climb.

Teachers reminded us constantly of what was at stake. Parents spoke in softer, more serious voices at dinner tables. The world around us seemed to be whispering the same thing: "Focus. Prepare. Grow up."

And we did try. We opened our books more often. We took notes, attended extra classes, revised late into the night. But somewhere between the pages of textbooks and the deadlines of assignments, our hearts still clung to the fading magic of school life. We still found excuses to stay a little longer after school. We still laughed over silly things that didn't matter but somehow meant everything. We still celebrated small victories like winning a friendly match or surprising a teacher on her birthday. We still found reasons to make memories, even as the clock ticked louder, reminding us that soon, this too would end.

Every event felt heavier now, wrapped in a strange sweetness and sadness all at once. Winning a medal at the last sports event felt less about victory and more about leaving a mark behind. Standing under the spotlight on the last annual day wasn't about performance anymore—it was about soaking in the feeling of being together one final time. Every festival, every decorated classroom, every casual conversation in the corridors carried a quiet ache beneath it—a knowledge that this life we had always known was breathing its final days.

And yet, even with the growing pressure, even with the looming goodbyes, we lived those days with a fullness we had never known before. Because we understood now—more deeply than ever—that moments are fleeting. That memories are built not in grand occasions, but in ordinary days made extraordinary by the people you spend them with. We held on to every small celebration, every group photo, every inside joke, every hurried lunch shared between classes, as if our hearts were trying to stitch together a memory big enough to carry into the unknown future.

This final year was not just the end of school. It was the end of a version of ourselves we would never meet again. The end of a time when dreams were innocent, when friendships were effortless, when life was simple. We were standing on the edge of something vast and uncertain, ready or not. And all we could do was take one last deep breath, one last lingering look, and step forward into the world waiting beyond those familiar gates.

And then came the farewell.

The final gathering.

The day that had lived in our imaginations for years, the day we had spoken about casually, jokingly, as something far away—suddenly standing right in front of us. And it didn't feel anything like we thought it would. It wasn't grand or movie-like. It was quiet. Heavy. Bittersweet. The decorations around the hall sparkled under the soft yellow lights, the laughter of students echoed in little bursts here and there, the teachers stood smiling gently at a distance—but behind it all was a silence none of us could escape. A silence that whispered, "This is the end of something you'll never get back."

We moved through the crowded hall that day with hearts heavier than our smiles showed. We looked for familiar faces in the crowd—faces we had seen nearly every day for years, faces that had grown up beside us without us even realizing it. We found each other in small groups, clinging together, taking hurried photographs, trying to capture a lifetime into a single frozen frame. Phone cameras flashed, arms thrown around each other's shoulders, eyes sparkling with a mixture of wild laughter and hidden tears. We knew these pictures wouldn't just be photos for us. They would be anchors to a time we would never want to forget.

Every hug lingered longer than usual. No one wanted to let go first. You could feel it—the tightening grip, the quiet sighs, the unspoken fear—"When will we meet again like this?" Some of us tried to laugh it off, cracking jokes a little too loudly, while others grew quieter, eyes darting around, memorizing every corner, every color, every voice, as if carving it deep into memory before it faded. We laughed till our stomachs hurt, then wiped away tears quickly when we thought no one was watching. We danced like children, not caring about the clumsy moves, because we were not dancing for fun. We were dancing against the ticking clock.

The teachers, who had been silent witnesses to our growing up, watched us with a tenderness that words could never fully capture. They had seen us in every season—our brightest moments and our clumsiest stumbles, our victories and our failures.

And as the evening slipped into night, and one by one the lights dimmed and the laughter quieted, there came the hardest part—saying goodbye. Real goodbye. Hugging friends with a tightness that words could not match, looking into eyes that had once been filled only with mischief, now glistening with something much deeper. Promising to stay in touch, to meet again soon, fully knowing that life has its way of making promises difficult to keep.

We took one last walk through the school corridors—the ones that had witnessed every version of ourselves. We paused at the empty classrooms, stood silently at the corners where we had once raced each other, leaned against the railings where we had once whispered secrets. Every crack in the wall, every scratch on the desk, every broken bench told a story—and for one last night, it all belonged to us.

Farewell wasn't a grand goodbye.
It was a slow breaking.
A silent carrying away of pieces of a life we loved too much to leave behind. It was smiling through the ache, laughing through the longing, hugging through the heartbreak.
And though we walked out of those school gates that night, we left a part of ourselves behind — forever tucked away in the hallways, the classrooms, the playgrounds, and in each other.

And just like that, the story that had been written across the walls of our childhood came to its quiet, trembling end. From the early chapters filled with innocent laughter, scraped knees, secret handshakes, and dreams too big for our tiny hands to hold — we grew. We lived through days when life was nothing but morning bells and stolen moments of joy, never imagining it could ever be any different. Then came the chapter we never saw coming — when the world fell silent, when classrooms became glowing screens, when friendships survived not through touch, but through memory and hope. We learned to wait, to long, to ache for ordinary days we once rushed through without a second thought. And when the gates finally reopened, we stepped into a world that looked the same, yet felt so painfully different. Faces had changed. Voices had changed. And somewhere deep inside, so had we.

We tried to pick up the pieces. We learned to laugh again, to play again, to chase the forgotten sunlight. But life, in its quiet way, reminded us to grow up. The push to take studies seriously came knocking, even when all our hearts wanted was a little more time to be reckless, to be young, to be free. We juggled dreams and deadlines, clung to friendships that felt more fragile now, more precious. And before we could even catch our breath, we found ourselves writing the final chapters — the last sports events, the last cheers echoing across empty fields, the last annual days spent under stage lights that seemed a little softer, a little sadder.

Then came farewell — a word too small for the heartbreak it carried. We searched for each other in the crowd, hugged a little longer, smiled a little wider, took photographs we knew would one day make our hearts ache in ways we couldn't yet understand. We laughed with voices that shook, promised to stay in touch even as we knew life had its way of pulling people apart. We danced not because it was tradition, but because it was survival — one last wild attempt to hold onto everything we loved before the world changed us too much.

And so, this is how it ends — not with a final bell, not with grand goodbyes, but with a thousand tiny moments stitched into the corners of our hearts forever. This was never just about school, about exams, about report cards. It was about becoming. About finding laughter after loss, about holding onto each other in the dark, about growing up even when we weren't ready.

Though the school gates have closed behind us, the echoes will live on — in the way we chase our dreams, in the friendships that outgrow distances, in the part of us that still believes in magic, no matter how much the world tries to make us forget.
And somewhere, in the quiet spaces of our hearts, the chapters of our school life will always keep breathing — soft, golden, untouched by time.

35

"No matter how many roads we take,
no matter how far our footsteps stray,
a piece of us will forever wander
the old corridors we once called home."

The End

About The Author.

Guthadar Mohammed Zarar is a storyteller of moments — the quiet, fleeting ones that often go unnoticed but leave the deepest imprints on our hearts.

His debut book, *In the Halls of Quiet Storms*, is more than just a recollection of school life — it is a tender tribute to the two unforgettable years he spent at **Montessori High School, India.** There, in those corridors echoing with laughter and the hush of farewell tears, Zarar found the memories that would later form the soul of his writing. Every chapter reflects a truth he holds close: school life, in all its chaos and charm, is a once-in-a-lifetime blessing — one we only understand fully once it slips into memory.

Zarar began his academic journey at MES Indian School in Doha, Qatar, where he first discovered the power of language. As an IEO Gold Medalist, he has always been enchanted by how words can cast spells — how language, in his words, "has its own magic that can gently sway hearts and quietly deceive the soul."

His writing is marked by an intimate, nostalgic voice — one that draws strength from simplicity, and emotion from silence. Through each line, he seeks to capture the unspoken — the friendships that shaped us, the dreams that stirred within classroom walls, and the bittersweet goodbyes we never truly prepared for.

With a pen guided by memory and a heart rooted in gratitude, Zarar continues to write — not just to tell stories, but to relive them, to honor them, and to remind us all that some places never really leave us. They live on, quietly, in the background of every step we take.

This is just the beginning of his journey — and many more stories are waiting to find their voice through him.

www.ingramcontent.com/pod-product-compliance
Lightning Source LLC
Chambersburg PA
CBHW020516160726
47991CB00007B/2985